THE

JOURNALS

OF

SUSANNA

MOODIE

The Journals of Susanna Moodie

Poems by

MARGARET ATWOOD

Toronto, Oxford University Press

Oxford University Press
70 Wynford Drive, Don Mills, Ontario M3C 1J9

Oxford New York
Athens Auckland Bangkok Bombay
Calcutta Cape Town Dar es Salaam Delhi
Florence Hong Kong Istanbul Karachi
Kuala Lumpur Madras Madrid Melbourne
Mexico City Nairobi Paris Singapore
Taipei Tokyo Toronto

and associated companies in
Berlin Ibadan

Oxford is a trademark of Oxford University Press

The collages and cover design
are by Margaret Atwood

20 21 22 — 99 98
Printed and bound in Canada
by Hignell Printing Limited

CONTENTS

JOURNAL I

JOURNAL II

JOURNAL III

AFTERWORD   62

I take this picture of myself
and with my sewing scissors
cut out the face.

Now it is more accurate:

where my eyes were,
every-
thing appears

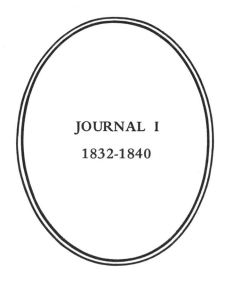

JOURNAL I

1832-1840

DISEMBARKING AT QUEBEC

Is it my clothes, my way of walking,
the things I carry in my hand
—a book, a bag with knitting--
the incongruous pink of my shawl

this space cannot hear

or is it my own lack
of conviction which makes
these vistas of desolation,
long hills, the swamps, the barren sand, the glare
of sun on the bone-white
driftlogs, omens of winter,
the moon alien in day-
time a thin refusal

The others leap, shout

    Freedom!

The moving water will not show me
my reflection.

The rocks ignore.

I am a word
in a foreign language.

FURTHER ARRIVALS

After we had crossed the long illness
that was the ocean, we sailed up-river

On the first island
the immigrants threw off their clothes
and danced like sandflies

We left behind one by one
the cities rotting with cholera,
one by one our civilized
distinctions

and entered a large darkness.

It was our own
ignorance we entered.

I have not come out yet

My brain gropes nervous
tentacles in the night, sends out
fears hairy as bears,
demands lamps; or waiting

for my shadowy husband, hears
malice in the trees' whispers.

I need wolf's eyes to see
the truth.

I refuse to look in a mirror.

Whether the wilderness is
real or not
depends on who lives there.

FIRST NEIGHBOURS

The people I live among, unforgivingly
previous to me, grudging
the way I breathe their
property, the air,
speaking a twisted dialect to my differently-
shaped ears

though I tried to adapt

(the girl in a red tattered
petticoat, who jeered at me for my burned bread

Go back where you came from

I tightened my lips; knew that England
was now unreachable, had sunk down into the sea
without ever teaching me about washtubs)

got used to being
a minor invalid, expected to make
inept remarks,
futile and spastic gestures

(asked the Indian
about the squat thing on a stick
drying by the fire: Is that a toad?
Annoyed, he said No no,
deer liver, very good)

Finally I grew a chapped tarpaulin
skin; I negotiated the drizzle
of strange meaning, set it
down to just the latitude:
something to be endured
but not surprised by.

Inaccurate. The forest can still trick me:
one afternoon while I was drawing
birds, a malignant face
flickered over my shoulder;
the branches quivered.

     Resolve: to be both tentative and hard to startle
     (though clumsiness and
     fright are inevitable)

     in this area where my damaged
     knowing of the language means
     prediction is forever impossible

THE PLANTERS

They move between the jagged edge
of the forest and the jagged river
on a stumpy patch of cleared land

my husband, a neighbour, another man
weeding the few rows
of string beans and dusty potatoes.

They bend, straighten; the sun
lights up their faces and hands, candles
flickering in the wind against the

unbright earth. I see them; I know
none of them believe they are here.
They deny the ground they stand on,

pretend this dirt is the future.
And they are right. If they let go
of that illusion solid to them as a shovel,

open their eyes even for a moment
to these trees, to this particular sun
they would be surrounded, stormed, broken

in upon by branches, roots, tendrils, the dark
side of light
as I am.

THE WEREMAN

My husband walks in the frosted field
an X, a concept
defined against a blank;
he swerves, enters the forest
and is blotted out.

Unheld by my sight
what does he change into
what other shape
blends with the under-
growth, wavers across the pools
is camouflaged from the listening
swamp animals

At noon he will
return; or it may be
only my idea of him
I will find returning
with him hiding behind it.

He may change me also
with the fox eye, the owl
eye, the eightfold
eye of the spider

I can't think
what he will see
when he opens the door

PATHS AND THINGSCAPE

Those who went ahead
of us in the forest
bent the early trees
so that they grew to signals:

the trail was not
among the trees but
the trees

and there are some who have dreams
of birds flying in the shapes
of letters; the sky's
codes;
       and dream also
the significance of numbers (count
petals of certain flowers)

       In the morning I advance
       through the doorway: the sun
       on the bark, the inter-
       twisted branches, here
       a blue movement in the leaves, dispersed
       calls/ no trails; rocks
       and grey tufts of moss

The petals of the fire-
weed fall where they fall

I am watched like an invader
who knows hostility but
not where

The day shrinks back from me

When will be
that union and each
thing (bits
of surface broken by my foot
step) will without moving move
around me
into its place

THE TWO FIRES

One, the summer fire
outside: the trees melting, returning
to their first red elements
on all sides, cutting me off
from escape or the saving
lake

I sat in the house, raised up
between that shapeless raging
and my sleeping children
a charm: concentrate on
form, geometry, the human
architecture of the house, square
closed doors, proved roofbeams,
the logic of windows

(the children could not be wakened:
in their calm dreaming
the trees were straight and still
had branches and were green)

The other, the winter
fire inside: the protective roof
shrivelling overhead, the rafters
incandescent, all those corners
and straight lines flaming, the carefully-
made structure
prisoning us in a cage of blazing
bars
        the children
were awake and crying;

I wrapped them, carried them
outside into the snow.
Then I tried to rescue
what was left of their scorched dream
about the house: blankets,
warm clothes, the singed furniture
of safety cast away with them
in a white chaos

Two fires in-
formed me,

(each refuge fails
us; each danger
becomes a haven)

left charred marks
now around which I
try to grow

LOOKING IN A MIRROR

It was as if I woke
after a sleep of seven years

to find stiff lace, religious
black rotted
off by earth and the strong waters

and instead my skin thickened
with bark and the white hairs of roots

My heirloom face I brought
with me a crushed eggshell
among other debris:
the china plate shattered
on the forest road, the shawl
from India decayed, pieces of letters

and the sun here had stained
me its barbarous colour

Hands grown stiff, the fingers
brittle as twigs
eyes bewildered after
seven years, and almost
blind/ buds, which can see
only the wind

the mouth cracking
open like a rock in fire
trying to say

What is this

(you find only
the shape you already are
but what
if you have forgotten that
or discover you
have never known)

DEPARTURE FROM THE BUSH

I, who had been erased
by fire, was crept in
upon by green
                    (how
lucid a season)

            In time the animals
arrived to inhabit me,

first one
  by one, stealthily
(their habitual traces
burnt); then
having marked new boundaries
returning, more
confident, year
by year, two
by two

but restless: I was not ready
altogether to be moved into

They could tell I was
too heavy: I might
capsize;

I was frightened
by their eyes (green or
amber) glowing out from inside me

I was not completed; at night
I could not see without lanterns.

He wrote, We are leaving. I said
I have no clothes
left I can wear

The snow came. The sleigh was a relief;
its track lengthened behind,
pushing me towards the city

and rounding the first hill, I was
(instantaneous)
unlived in: they had gone.

There was something they almost taught me
I came away not having learned.

JOURNAL II

1840-1871

DEATH OF A YOUNG SON BY DROWNING

He, who navigated with success
the dangerous river of his own birth
once more set forth

on a voyage of discovery
into the land I floated on
but could not touch to claim.

His feet slid on the bank,
the currents took him;
he swirled with ice and trees in the swollen water

and plunged into distant regions,
his head a bathysphere;
through his eyes' thin glass bubbles

he looked out, reckless adventurer
on a landscape stranger than Uranus
we have all been to and some remember.

There was an accident; the air locked,
he was hung in the river like a heart.
They retrieved the swamped body,

cairn of my plans and future charts,
with poles and hooks
from among the nudging logs.

It was spring, the sun kept shining, the new grass
lept to solidity;
my hands glistened with details.

After the long trip I was tired of waves.
My foot hit rock. The dreamed sails
collapsed, ragged.

      I planted him in this country
      like a flag.

THE IMMIGRANTS

They are allowed to inherit
the sidewalks involved as palmlines, bricks
exhausted and soft, the deep
lawnsmells, orchards whorled
to the land's contours, the inflected weather

only to be told they are too poor
to keep it up, or someone
has noticed and wants to kill them; or the towns
pass laws which declare them obsolete.

I see them coming
up from the hold smelling of vomit,
infested, emaciated, their skins grey
with travel; as they step on shore

the old countries recede, become
perfect, thumbnail castles preserved
like gallstones in a glass bottle, the
towns dwindle upon the hillsides
in a light paperweight-clear.

They carry their carpetbags and trunks
with clothes, dishes, the family pictures;
they think they will make an order
like the old one, sow miniature orchards,
carve children and flocks out of wood

but always they are too poor, the sky
is flat, the green fruit shrivels
in the prairie sun, wood is for burning;
and if they go back, the towns

in time have crumbled, their tongues
stumble among awkward teeth, their ears
are filled with the sound of breaking glass.
I wish I could forget them
and so forget myself:

my mind is a wide pink map
across which move year after year
arrows and dotted lines, further and further,
people in railway cars

their heads stuck out of the windows
at stations, drinking milk or singing,
their features hidden with beards or shawls
day and night riding across an ocean of unknown
land to an unknown land.

DREAM 1: THE BUSH GARDEN

I stood once more in that garden
sold, deserted and
gone to seed

In the dream I could
see down through the earth, could see
the potatoes curled
like pale grubs in the soil
the radishes thrusting down
their fleshy snouts, the beets
pulsing like slow amphibian hearts

Around my feet
the strawberries were surging, huge
and shining

When I bent
to pick, my hands
came away red and wet

In the dream I said
I should have known
anything planted here
would come up blood

1837 WAR IN RETROSPECT

One of the
things I found out by being
there, and after:

that history (that list
of ballooning wishes, flukes,
bent times, plunges and mistakes
clutched like parachutes)

is rolling itself up in your head
at one end and unrolling at the other

that this war will soon be among
those tiny ancestral figures
flickering dull white through the back of your skull,
confused, anxious, not sure any more
what they are doing there

appearing from time to time
with idiot faces and hands clusters
of bananas, holding flags,
holding guns, advancing through the trees
brown line green scribble

or crouching within a rough grey
crayon diagram of a fort,
shooting at each other, the smoke and red fire
made actual through a child's fingers.

DREAM 2: BRIAN THE STILL-HUNTER

The man I saw in the forest
used to come to our house
every morning, never said anything;
I learned from the neighbours later
he once tried to cut his throat.

I found him at the end of the path
sitting on a fallen tree
cleaning his gun.

There was no wind;
around us the leaves rustled.

He said to me:
I kill because I have to

but every time I aim, I feel
my skin grow fur
my head heavy with antlers
and during the stretched instant
the bullet glides on its thread of speed
my soul runs innocent as hooves.

Is God just to his creatures?

I die more often than many.

He looked up and I saw
the white scar made by the hunting knife
around his neck.

When I woke
I remembered: he has been gone
twenty years and not heard from.

CHARIVARI

'They capped their heads with feathers, masked
their faces, wore their clothes backwards, howled
with torches through the midnight winter

and dragged the black man from his house
to the jolting music of broken
instruments, pretending to each other

it was a joke, until
they killed him. I don't know
what happened to the white bride.'

The American lady, adding she
thought it was a disgraceful piece
of business, finished her tea.

(Note: Never pretend this isn't
part of the soil too, teadrinkers, and inadvertent
victims and murderers, when we come this way

again in other forms, take care
to look behind, within
where the skeleton face beneath

the face puts on its feather mask, the arm
within the arm lifts up the spear:
Resist those cracked

drumbeats. Stop this. Become human.)

DREAM 3: NIGHT BEAR
WHICH FRIGHTENED CATTLE

Horns crowding toward us
a stampede of bellowing, one
night the surface of my mind keeps
only as anecdote

We laughed, safe with lanterns
at the kitchen door

though beneath stories

where forgotten birds
tremble through memory, ripples across water
and a moon hovers in the lake
orange and prehistoric

I lean with my feet grown intangible
because I am not there

watching the bear I didn't see condense
itself among the trees, an outline
tenuous as an echo

but it is real, heavier
than real   I know
even by daylight here
in this visible kitchen

it absorbs all terror

it moves toward the lighted cabin
below us on the slope
where my family gathers

a mute vibration passing
between my ears

THE DEATHS OF THE OTHER CHILDREN

The body dies

little by little

the body buries itself

joins itself
to the loosened mind, to the black-
berries and thistles, running in a
thorny wind
over the shallow
foundations of our former houses,
dim hollows now in the sandy soil

Did I spend all those years
building up this edifice
my composite
                self, this crumbling hovel?

My arms, my eyes, my grieving
words, my disintegrated children

Everywhere I walk, along
the overgrowing paths, my skirt
tugged at by the spreading briers

they catch at my heels with their fingers

THE DOUBLE VOICE

Two voices
took turns using my eyes:

One had manners,
painted in watercolours,
used hushed tones when speaking
of mountains or Niagara Falls,
composed uplifting verse
and expended sentiment upon the poor.

The other voice
had other knowledge:
that men sweat
always and drink often,
that pigs are pigs
but must be eaten
anyway, that unborn babies
fester like wounds in the body,
that there is nothing to be done
about mosquitoes;

One saw through my
bleared and gradually
bleaching eyes, red leaves,
the rituals of seasons and rivers

The other found a dead dog
jubilant with maggots
half-buried among the sweet peas.

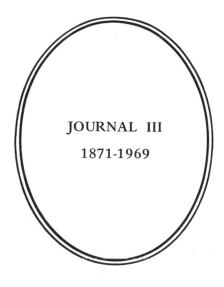

JOURNAL III

1871-1969

LATER IN BELLEVILLE: CAREER

Once by a bitter candle
of oil and braided
rags, I wrote
verses about love and sleighbells

which I exchanged for potatoes;

in the summers I painted butterflies
on a species of white fungus
which were bought by the tourists, glass-
cased for English parlours

and my children (miraculous)
wore shoes.

Now every day
I sit on a stuffed sofa
in my own fringed parlour, have
uncracked plates (from which I eat
at intervals)
and a china teaset.

There is no use for art.

DAGUERREOTYPE TAKEN IN OLD AGE

I know I change
have changed

but whose is this vapid face
pitted and vast, rotund
suspended in empty paper
as though in a telescope

the granular moon

I rise from my chair
pulling against gravity
I turn away
and go out into the garden

I revolve among the vegetables,
my head ponderous
reflecting the sun
in shadows from the pocked ravines
cut in my cheeks, my eye-
sockets 2 craters

along the paths
I orbit
the apple trees
white white spinning
stars around me

I am being
eaten away by light

WISH: METAMORPHOSIS
TO HERALDIC EMBLEM

I balance myself carefully
inside my shrinking body
which is nevertheless
deceptive as a cat's fur:

when I am dipped in the earth
I will be much smaller.

On my skin the wrinkles branch
out, overlapping like hair or feathers.

In this parlour my grandchildren
uneasy on sunday chairs
with my deafness, my cameo brooch
my puckered mind
scurrying in its old burrows

little guess how
                maybe

I will prowl and slink
in crystal darkness
among the stalactite roots, with new
formed plumage
                uncorroded
                      gold and

Fiery green, my fingers
curving and scaled, my

opal
    no
  eyes glowing

VISIT TO TORONTO, WITH COMPANIONS

The streets are new, the harbour
is new also;
the lunatic asylum is yellow.

On the first floor there were
women sitting, sewing;
they looked at us sadly, gently,
answered questions.

On the second floor there were
women crouching, thrashing,
tearing off their clothes, screaming;
to us they paid little attention.

On the third floor
I went through a glass-panelled
door into a different kind of room.
It was a hill, with boulders, trees, no houses.
I sat down and smoothed my gloves.

The landscape was saying something
but I couldn't hear. One of the rocks
sighed and rolled over.

Above me, at eye level
three faces appeared in an oblong space.

They wanted me to go out
to where there were streets and
the Toronto harbour

I shook my head. There were no clouds, the flowers
deep red and feathered, shot from among
the dry stones,
                    the air
was about to tell me
all kinds of answers

SOLIPSISM WHILE DYING

the skeleton produces flesh   enemy
opposing, then taken
for granted, earth harvested, used
up, walked over

the ears produce sounds   what I heard I
created. (voices
determining, repeating
histories, worn customs

the mouth produces words   I said I created
myself, and these
frames, commas, calendars
that enclose me

the hands produce objects   the world touched
into existence: was
this cup, this village here
before my fingers

the eyes produce light   the sky
leaps at me: let there be
the sun-
set

Or so I thought, lying in the bed
being regretted

added: What will they do now
that I, that all
depending on me disappears?

Where will be Belleville?

      Kingston?

      (the fields
       I held between. the lake
      boats

          t o r o N T O

THOUGHTS FROM UNDERGROUND

When I first reached this country
I hated it
and I hated it more each year:

in summer the light a
violent blur, the heat
thick as a swamp,
the green things fiercely
shoving themselves upwards, the
eyelids bitten by insects

In winter our teeth were brittle
with cold. We fed on squirrels.
At night the house cracked.
In the mornings, we thawed
the bad bread over the stove.

Then we were made successful
and I felt I ought to love
this country.
                I said I loved it
and my mind saw double.

I began to forget myself
in the middle
of sentences. Events
were split apart

I fought. I constructed
desperate paragraphs of praise, everyone
ought to love it because

and set them up at intervals

        due to natural resources, native industry, superior
        penitentiaries
        we will all be rich and powerful

flat as highway billboards

        who can doubt it, look how
        fast Belleville is growing

(though it is still no place for an english gentleman)

ALTERNATE THOUGHTS
FROM UNDERGROUND

Down. Shovelled. Can hear
faintly laughter, footsteps;
the shrill of glass and steel

the invaders of those for whom
shelter was wood,
fire was terror and sacred

the inheritors, the raisers
of glib superstructures.

My heart silted by decades
of older thoughts, yet prays

O topple this glass pride, fireless
rivetted babylon, prays
through subsoil
to my wooden fossil God.

But they prevail. Extinct. I feel
scorn but also pity: what
the bones of the giant reptiles

done under by the thing
(may call it
climate) outside the circle
they drew by their closed senses
of what was right

felt when scuttled
across, nested in by the velvet immoral
uncalloused and armourless mammals.

RESURRECTION

I see now I see
now I cannot see

earth is a blizzard in my eyes

I hear now

        the rustle of the snow

the angels listening above me

        thistles bright with sleet
        gathering

waiting for the time
to reach me
up to the pillared
sun, the final city

        or living towers

unrisen yet
whose dormant stones lie folding
their holy fire around me

       (but the land shifts with frost
        and those who have become the stone
        voices of the land
        shift also and say

        god is not
        the voice in the whirlwind

        god is the whirlwind

        at the last
        judgement we will all be trees

A BUS ALONG ST CLAIR: DECEMBER

It would take more than that to banish
me: this is my kingdom still.

Turn, look up
through the gritty window: an unexplored
wilderness of wires

Though they buried me in monuments
of concrete slabs, of cables
though they mounded a pyramid
of cold light over my head
though they said, We will build
silver paradise with a bulldozer

it shows how little they know
about vanishing: I have
my ways of getting through.

Right now, the snow
is no more familiar
to you than it was to me:
this is my doing.
The grey air, the roar
going on behind it
are no more familiar.

I am the old woman
sitting across from you on the bus,
her shoulders drawn up like a shawl;
out of her eyes come secret
hatpins, destroying
the walls, the ceiling

Turn, look down:
there is no city;
this is the centre of a forest

your place is empty

61

AFTERWORD

These poems were generated by a dream. I dreamt I was watching an opera I had written about Susanna Moodie. I was alone in the theatre; on the empty white stage, a single figure was singing.

Although I had heard of Susanna Moodie I had never read her two books about Canada, *Roughing It in the Bush* and *Life in the Clearings*. When I did read them I was disappointed. The prose was discursive and ornamental and the books had little shape: they were collections of disconnected anecdotes. The only thing that held them together was the personality of Mrs Moodie, and what struck me most about this personality was the way in which it reflects many of the obsessions still with us.

If the national mental illness of the United States is megalomania, that of Canada is paranoid schizophrenia. Mrs Moodie is divided down the middle: she praises the Canadian landscape but accuses it of destroying her; she dislikes the people already in Canada but finds in people her only refuge from the land itself; she preaches progress and the march of civilization while brooding elegiacally upon the destruction of the wilderness; she delivers optimistic sermons while showing herself to be fascinated with deaths, murders, the criminals in Kingston Penitentiary and the incurably insane in the Toronto lunatic asylum. She claims to be an ardent Canadian patriot while all the time she is standing back from the country and criticizing it as though she were a detached observer, a stranger. Perhaps that is the way we still live. We are all immigrants to this place even if we were born here: the country is too big for anyone to inhabit completely, and in the parts unknown to us we move in fear, exiles and invaders. This country is something that must be chosen--it is so easy to leave--and if we do choose it we are still choosing a violent duality.

This is a modified version of a radio-broadcast introduction.

Once I had read the books I forgot about them. The poems occurred later, over a period of a year and a half. I suppose many of them were suggested by Mrs Moodie's books, though it was not her conscious voice but the other voice running like a counterpoint through her work that made the most impression on me. Although the poems can be read in connection with Mrs Moodie's books, they don't have to be: they have detached themselves from the books in the same way that other poems detach themselves from the events that give rise to them.

The arrangement of the poems follows, more or less, the course of Mrs Moodie's life. Journal I begins with her arrival in Canada and her voyage up the St Lawrence, past Quebec and Montreal where a cholera epidemic is raging. In Upper Canada she encounters earlier settlers who despise the Moodies as greenhorns and cheat them whenever possible. Later, on a remote bush farm, she can neither hold on to her English past nor renounce it for a belief in her Canadian future. After seven years of struggle and near starvation, and just as she is beginning to come to terms with her environment, the family moves away.

After 1840 the Moodies lived in Belleville, where Susanna's husband had been made sheriff as a result of his helping to suppress the rebellion of 1837. (Ironically, Susanna later admitted that the rebellion was probably a good thing for Canada.) Journal II contains reflections about the society Mrs Moodie finds herself in, as well as memories of the years spent in the bush. At the beginning of this section Mrs Moodie finally accepts the reality of the country she is in, and at its end she accepts also the inescapable doubleness of her own vision.

Most of Journal III was written after I had come across a little-known photograph of Susanna Moodie as a mad-looking and very elderly lady. The poems take her through an estranged old age, into death and beyond. After her death she can hear the twentieth century above

her, bulldozing away her past, but she refuses to be
ploughed under completely. She makes her final appear-
ance in the present, as an old woman on a Toronto bus
who reveals the city as an unexplored, threatening
wilderness. Susanna Moodie has finally turned herself
inside out, and has become the spirit of the land she
once hated.